# Everglades
## National Park

### by Mike Graf

**Consultant:**
David Szymanski
Supervisory Park Ranger
Science Education and Outreach
Everglades National Park

# Bridgestone Books
an imprint of Capstone Press
Mankato, Minnesota

Bridgestone Books are published by Capstone Press
151 Good Counsel Drive, P.O. Box 669, Mankato, Minnesota 56002
http://www.capstone-press.com

*Library of Congress Cataloging-in-Publication Data*
Graf, Mike.
    Everglades National Park/by Mike Graf.
    v. cm.—(National parks)
    Includes bibliographical references (p. 23) and index.
    Contents: Everglades National Park—How the Everglades formed—People in the
Everglades—Weather—Plants—Animals—Activities—Safety—Park Issues—Map activity—
About national parks—Glossary
    ISBN 0-7368-2219-4 (hardcover)
    1. Everglades National Park (Fla.)—Juvenile literature. [1. Everglades National Park (Fla.)
2. National parks and reserves.] I. Title. II. Series: Graf, Mike. National parks.
F317.E9G73  2004
917.59'390464—dc21                                                    2002154604

**Editorial Credits**
Christianne C. Jones, editor; Linda Clavel, series designer; Enoch Peterson, book designer;
    Anne McMullen, illustrator; Alta Schaffer, photo researcher; Karen Risch,
    product planning editor

**Photo Credits**
Corbis/Kevin Fleming, 8
Danilo Donadoni/Bruce Coleman Inc., 14
Houserstock/Dave G. Houser, 1; Jan Butchofsky-Houser, 17
James P. Rowan, 6, 12
Mark Allen Stack/Tom Stack & Associates, 18
Tom & Pat Leeson, cover, 16
Tom Till, 4, 10

1 2 3 4 5 6 08 07 06 05 04 03

# Table of Contents

Florida

# Everglades National Park

Everglades National Park is a huge area of water and grass. A large river slowly flows through the Everglades. The river is miles wide but only inches deep. American Indians called the area "Pa-hay-okee." It means "grassy waters." Many plants and animals make up this ecosystem.

Everglades National Park is part of the Florida Everglades. In 1947, the U.S. government set aside part of the Everglades as a national park. The park covers 1,509,000 acres (610,692 hectares) of land in southern Florida. It is one-seventh of the entire Everglades area.

The government creates national parks to protect natural areas. People can camp, hike, and view the scenery in these areas. But they cannot build or hunt on park lands. More than 1 million people visit Everglades National Park each year.

**Water and saw-grass cover most of Everglades National Park.**

In the past 2 million years, southern Florida has been above and below sea level. Sea level is the average surface level of the world's oceans. The water level of the oceans changes with the warm and cool periods on Earth.

Millions of years ago, glaciers covered most of North America. The glaciers held a lot of water. The ocean's water level rose when the glaciers melted.

Southern Florida was above sea level until the glaciers melted. The extra ocean water covered parts of southern Florida. Now the flat area of land that forms the Everglades is barely above sea level.

Limestone rocks make up the ground in the Everglades. Shells, mud, and sand hardened at the bottom of the ocean and formed limestone. Above this rock layer are the wetlands and grasslands that make up the Everglades.

**The limestone rock that forms the ground of the Everglades can often be seen during the dry season.**

# People in the Everglades

American Indians were the first people to come to the Everglades. They lived there at least 4,000 years ago. The earliest known people in the Everglades include the Tequesta and Calusa Indians.

In the early 1500s, Spanish explorers came to Florida looking for gold. They tried to set up missions to convert the Indians to Christianity. Many Indians left the Everglades area.

Loggers, miners, farmers, and railroad workers started to move to Florida in the 1800s. At this time, many Seminole Indians were living in the area. The new settlers wanted the Seminole to leave. Between 1817 and 1858, the United States and the Seminole fought three wars over the land.

During the 1900s, the Everglades began to see the effects of all the people moving into the area. The area was losing water and land. Marjory Stoneman Douglas was one of the first people to see the need to protect the area.

**Marjory Stoneman Douglas is called the "mother of the Everglades" because she helped protect the area.**

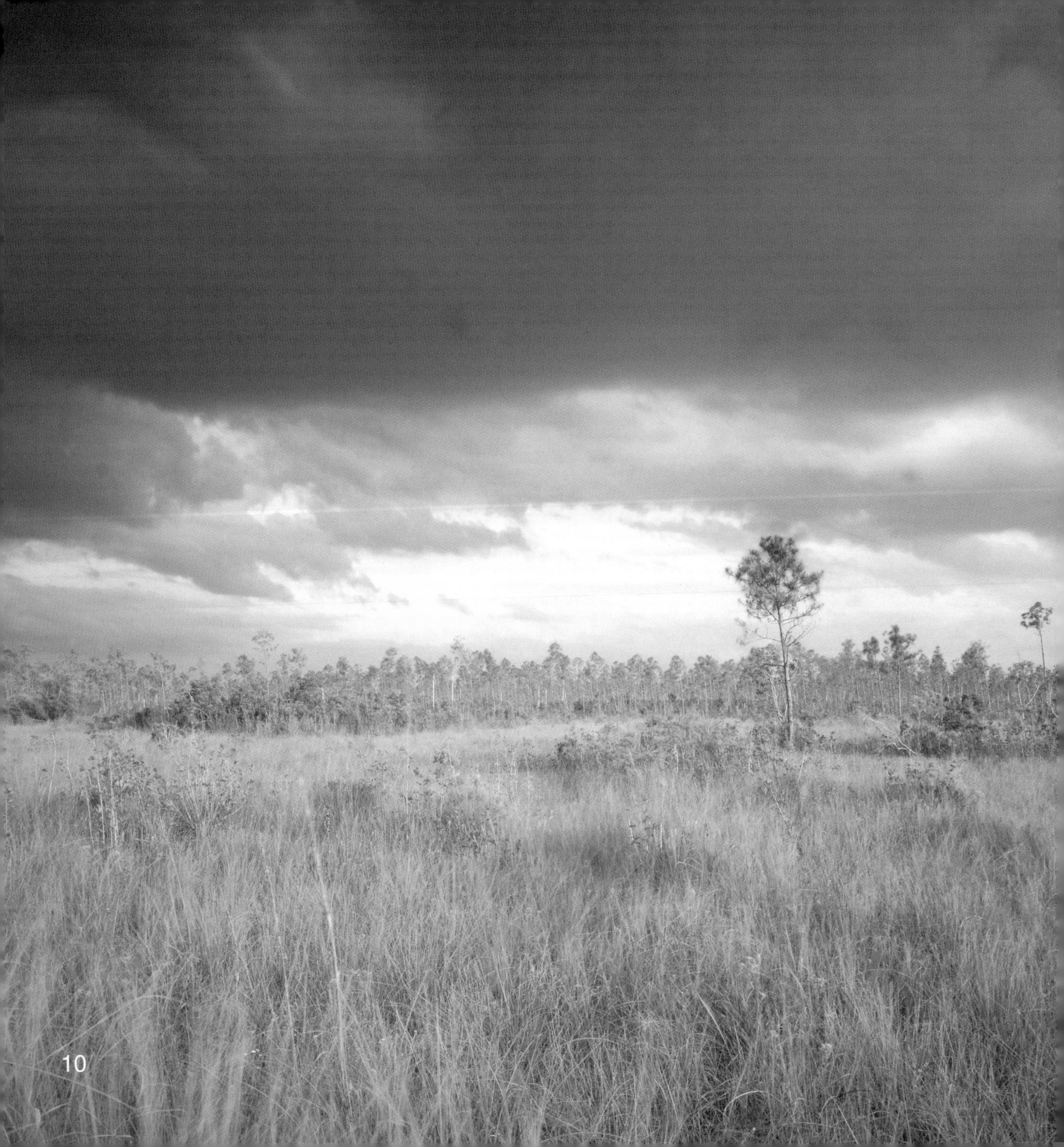

# Weather

The Everglades has two seasons. The rainy season begins in late May or June. It lasts through November. The dry season begins in December and lasts until April or May.

The rainy season is warm and humid. It is around 90 degrees Fahrenheit (32 degrees Celsius) during the day. The park receives most of its rain during this season. The Everglades gets 40 to 65 inches (100 to 165 centimeters) of rain each year.

Hurricanes can form during the rainy season. A hurricane is a strong wind and rain storm that starts on the ocean. Florida has more hurricanes than anywhere else in the United States.

December is the beginning of the dry season. Little rain falls during the next six to eight months. It is cooler and less humid during this time. The dry season is the best time to visit the park.

**Thunderstorms often cross the Everglades, giving Florida the nickname "Thunderstorm Capital of the United States."**

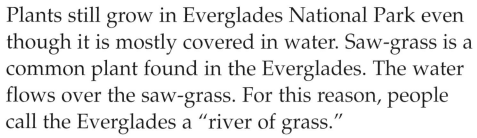

# Plants

Plants still grow in Everglades National Park even though it is mostly covered in water. Saw-grass is a common plant found in the Everglades. The water flows over the saw-grass. For this reason, people call the Everglades a "river of grass."

Many plants and trees grow on islands in the Everglades. Gumbo-limbo trees have red, peeling bark. They are nicknamed the "tourist tree" because they look like sunburned tourists. Strangler figs are also found on islands. Their small seeds grow on other trees. Strangler figs slowly strangle and crush the trees they grow on.

Mangrove forests grow in the southern part of the park. Mangrove forests are made up of red, black, and white mangrove trees. Mangrove trees grow best in tidal waters. Tidal waters are a mix of freshwater and salt water. The roots on mangrove trees grow above and below the ground. These roots are called prop roots.

**This strangler fig wraps itself around the trunk of another tree.**

Everglades National Park has many endangered animals. The Florida panther, the American crocodile, and the Florida manatee are a few endangered species that live in Everglades National Park.

The Everglades is known for its reptiles and amphibians. It is the only place in the world where both alligators and crocodiles live together. Turtles, frogs, and many types of snakes also live in the park.

More than 340 kinds of birds live in Everglades National Park. The great egret is one of the wading birds found in the park. Wading birds have long legs that help them walk through the shallow, muddy water. Flamingoes and storks are other common wading birds found in the park.

**The American crocodile is one of the endangered species protected in the Everglades.**

15

# Activities

Wildlife watching is one of the most popular activities at Everglades National Park. Wading birds can be seen in the Florida Bay. Both alligators and crocodiles can also be spotted in the park.

Canoeing, kayaking, and boating are other activities in Everglades National Park. Boat tours are given in different parts of the park. More daring visitors can paddle canoes on the Everglades' waterways. The park also has places for biking, hiking, and fishing.

# Safety

While at the park, visitors should stay on trails or viewing platforms for safety. Visitors should always listen to tour guides' directions and follow park rules. People need to be aware of dangerous animals while hiking. Poisonous snakes, crocodiles, and alligators are dangerous animals that live in the park.

Southern Florida is very hot and humid. People who visit the park should drink plenty of water and wear sunscreen.

# Park Issues

The Everglades' biggest problem is loss of water. The water loss is changing the park's ecosystem. It affects the park's plants and animals.

A canal system is draining the water from the area. The system was built after a major hurricane in 1947. The canals were designed to keep flood water out of the cities. But the canals also drain all the water around the cities. The canals started draining water from the Everglades.

The canals also change the water flow from Lake Okeechobee to the Everglades. The water from the lake is being used for other things. It is now used for drinking water and watering crops.

Park officials are trying to manage the Everglades' water supply. In 2000, Congress passed a bill to restore the water supply. This law will make sure the area gets enough water for the wildlife, the people, and the land.

**Irrigation canals disrupt the water flow from Lake Okeechobee to the Everglades.**

# Map Activity

Everglades National Park has a 99-mile (159-kilometer) Wilderness Waterway. This waterway winds from the Gulf Coast Visitor Center to the Flamingo Visitor Center. This route has many campsites. Try this activity to see how far it is from one campsite to another.

**What You Need**
Ruler
20-inch (51-centimeter) piece of string

**What You Do**
1. Find the Wilderness Waterway on the map. Pick a campsite along this route.
2. Using the ruler, measure the actual distance between the beginning of the route and the campsite. Use the map's scale to find the distance to this campsite.
3. Next, measure the distance you have to boat. Place one end of the string on the beginning of the waterway. Lay the string down following the winding path of the Wilderness Waterway until you reach your site.
4. With the ruler, measure the length of string you used. Use the scale to find the distance in miles or kilometers. Try this activity with several campsites along this route.

National Parks

Alaska

Hawaii

American Samoa

Puerto Rico

## About National Parks

The U.S. government creates national parks to protect natural areas. In 1916, the U.S. government formed the National Park Service. This group was created to oversee all U.S. park lands. The National Park Service runs nearly 400 areas. These sites include recreational areas, natural landmarks, and historic sites such as battlefields. Today, the United States has more than 50 national parks.

# Words to Know

**ecosystem** (EE-koh-siss-tuhm)—a community of animals and plants interacting with their environment

**endangered** (en-DAYN-jurd)—at risk of dying out

**glacier** (GLAY-shur)—a large, slow-moving sheet of ice and snow

**grasslands** (GRASS-landz)—large, open areas of grass

**humid** (HYOO-mid)—moist

**hurricane** (HUR-uh-kane)—a strong wind and rain storm that starts on the ocean

**sea level** (SEE LEV-uhl)—the average surface level of the world's oceans

**species** (SPEE-sheez)—a group of plants or animals that share common characteristics

**wetlands** (WET-landz)—areas of swamps or marshes

# Read More

**Furstinger, Nancy.** *Everglades.* Natural Wonders of the U.S.A. Mankato, Minn.: Weigl, 2003.

**Raatma, Lucia.** *Our National Parks.* Let's See. Minneapolis: Compass Point Books, 2002.

**Yolen, Jane.** *Welcome to the River of Grass.* New York: Putnam's, 2001.

# Useful Addresses

Everglades National Park
40001 State Road 9336
Homestead, FL  33034-6733

National Park Service
1849 C Street NW
Washington, DC  20240

# Internet Sites

Do you want to find out more about Everglades National Park?
Let FactHound, our fact-finding hound dog,
do the research for you.

Here's how:
1) Visit **http://www.facthound.com**
2) Type in the **Book ID** number: **0736822194**
3) Click on **FETCH IT**.

FactHound will fetch Internet sites picked
by our editors just for you!

# Index